Once
We Were
Giants

Kirsty
McHattie

Tasker Press

Once We Were Giants

Copyright © 2023 Kirsty McHattie
Published by Tasker Press

ISBN 978-1-80068-644-1

Printed and bound in Great Britain by:
ImprintDigital.com
Seychelles Farm
Upton Pyne EX5 5HY
www.imprintdigital.com
01392 851550

Typeset by:
Derek Hall
halderek@icloud.com

Cover photos:
Alexander McHattie

Author's contact:
Kirsty McHattie
kirstymchattie@gmail.com
07903 011890

"Every now and then, say 'what the fuck'.
'What the fuck' gives you freedom.
Freedom brings opportunity.
Opportunity makes your future".

'Risky Business',
1983 Dir. Paul Brickman

Places

Love, Jealousy & Obsession

Sex

Reminiscence & Yearning

'Once We Were Giants' is my second poetry anthology following 'The Wrecked Muscle' released in 2019. It includes new and older work chosen for the way the pieces slip against one another, with a couple that elbowed their way insistently into the mix - because that's life and you can't curate everything.

MMXXIII

Birches

Like the blooming of a little milk in black tea
sadness comes for me
rising in polite rage

Russian melancholy
creeps within my bones
a soreness for all time

Give me
a wooden shingled church
brightly lit
with a thousand flickering faces

Slumbering forests
of whitened birch,
skinny soldiers
reaching for sky

For three days
we rushed past them
in their thousands,
and they obscured the seam
of east and west.

In Crete

Lost in the land of the Minotaur.
Spreading riches widely, he runs
jumping peak-to-peak
claiming honey for muses,
gathering cleansing resins for the skin.

Fires burn, miles from all quenching.
They mesmerise, taunting the senses
fragrance on an already perfumed night.

At the point where Byzantium came calling
the stunted lighthouse plays at lookout,
a mini sentinel of no real means.

High away, in northern hills, I stand
a better view afforded by manicured windows.

Republic in my ear,
and all heaven in my eyes.

I wish I lived on the plains

I wish I lived on the plains.
Wide open to heaven,
the air heavy with rain and heat,
pulsing with promised thunder

A white-clad house,
an overhanging porch
clattering dilapidatedly,
elephantine sideboards within
storing my tragedies

Here comes the storm
still fifty miles away.
The rain begins
sultry heat rising from baked earth,
twists towards me like a lover.

The lights flicker
you hold me -
electricity kicking into slow hearts.

Then morning, sweeter than any before,
mercury climbing
edging towards ninety.

The grasses whisper of nothing
and everything,
sky soaring
to a cathedral of eternity.

I rest against a damp bale
lulled to sleep
by whispering mice within.

I wish I lived on the plains,
I wish I lived on the plains.

I didn't get the Lake District

Hot on the tail of the elusive beast
inspiration,
I travelled north

North, where colours mute
and transformative shadow
bends in dark light,
revealing the world as it really is,
as it once was

Hundreds of years,
rolling back time, boiling clouds
rushing over peaks in reverse.
A tiny tornado sucks in on itself,
and hundreds become thousands

Rain blackens the babies of volcanoes,
engorges forces with greater purpose
and cleanses every shred of vision
from my grasping, desperate mind.

Thousands become millions
I am stripped of incentive to try.
There is no ruination here,
no furious nor frantic need
to imagine past lives
in this managed place

High-vis toilers scuttle on mountainsides
carefully placing and re-placing rocks,
funnelling feet (and discovery)
on prescribed pathways

Only the mist,
a wreathing ribbon
creeping in glacial cut-throughs,
is permitted to explore

Nothing shatters but the slate
and the landscape does not turn inward
gnawing, determined to eat itself

It says more about me
than of the Lake District
that I would wrench out and offer
my super-heated heart
to see the mountains fall.

The Why

How can you know me?
You don't even see me
Eyes downcast, walking fast,
crossing roads to avoid me

The divide, so physical,
resides in us both
hip to hip,
we're impregnable

Static veils the noise of our silence
and our avowed shout:
'never the twain shall meet,
nor greet
or be greeted'

Such fleeting, a passing,
suffused yellow night
seeps between us
and buzzes in time
with rumbling ten wheelers
sirens, and rubber-laying racers

This solemn place shall be nibbled away,
scribbled over existence
of grey upon grey

Stacked up high, played like records
tracks of the past,
a history unmetered
not built to last

Remember,
once we were giants
our footprints trod deep
made their paths on this landscape
that we'll always keep

Though the paths may be barred
by the new or reborn
we remember the pathways
and how, despite scorn,
we loved, lived and laughed
made our homes in the sky.
And for me, you and us
right there is the why.

There is always a path

There is always a path
trodden-down grasses
thumped-through thistles
flattened in passing.

Inquisitorial, weaving our way,
spirals leading back from where they came
and shall likely never go again.

There is always a path
a river, a torrent,
cutting rock to kingdom come.

Haystacks
silent sentries
warming in the sun.

The Art of War

Underline me in the little black book
of your mind's eye,
tapping a pencil on your teeth
remembering,
the last time I saw your face
was the last time.

And there can be no desire
hotter, brighter, fitter
than obsession in miniature.

Dirty thoughts

Maybe thinking about it too much
made it real

Perhaps suspicion is the creator
and uncertainty the maker

To quote a well-worn platitude:
this is not my fault

Or is it?

In some small part,
fears crystalised, realised
just by being thought.

The weight of love

The weight of all you do for me
has made my back sore.

Muscles aching from your care.
The chafing of each deed
reddens my skin, and I scratch
asking for mercy.

I cannot take another straw
of your love for me, my love.
A single kind word
will break my back.

And, yes, I fear. Locked up in my head
for days and days
unending, unyielding
to the release of sorrow.

Why am I doing sixty crunches a night?
To withstand
the crushing, folding suffocation
of your adoration.

Ungrateful?
Yes, I must be.
Add ungrateful to my shopping basket
I'm buying.

I should have got a trolley,
but I didn't have a pound,
and now my arms are aching
as well as my back.

If there's an answer on the way
I heed it: faster! faster!
It must have feet of clay.

Love is too great a weight
for me to bear.

The industry of the poet

The industry of the poet is obsession
and if we turn our gaze upon you
expect to be stripped and jumbled,
gleaming in the light of scrutiny
your every facet illuminated

We expose, consequently
tearing ourselves apart,
a frenzy of discovery
burrowing into shame
as though it were an elixir

We tunnel, needful
searching in you
for what we desire
to be true of us

We lay awake
fitfully constructing
and moulding you
to ideals,
then curse inwardly
for imbuing you with gifts
or agonies
that you do not possess

And when we've used you
you become undone!
We've sicked up the part of you
that held us hostage,
empty of meaning.

We send you fluttering to the breeze.
Just words on a page
and an ache in our guts.

The see-through face

Bare faced, polished like a stone
gazing into pooling deformation,
rank with artifice
pulled as an oxen cart
over the furrows of time

The sighing heart
misted by sorrow
still bursts,
saddled in well-worn pride

A moving face echoes
with spells yet-to-be-cast
and deeds complicit
in a mighty downfall

Joannes and Sarahs
polluted my wants and wishes;
several of them became ash
sticking to wet skin.

A way to break a heart

Think about it
would it be so terrible?
The spoils of a war to be split

No-one carries the winner's flag,
if I did, it would break my back
I'm no rider on the storm
any more than I'm a poster girl for you

Throw it out.
Gather back the shattered remnants
sweep up what's left
and call it art

Or an experiment
a test of reserve
a nerve of steel
a way to break a heart

What's the worth
of a life gone to ruin
Decay, my favourite aesthetic
my life best lived was always a mess,
it's my way, my way
but let's not climb a Hollywood hill
for a view of what could have been

It never was a rosy tale
nor a highlight in the dark
a silly, idle freak of me
a way to break a heart,
a way to keep a spirit hot
and feel the heat
coming up from somewhere else,
across and beyond the spires,
and dreaming palaces of a mind
in touching distance of hell

Seeing in the dark
isn't just for cats.
It's for those who can't abide the light,
learning to read shadows
making sense of lumps and bumps
feeling our way along the landing,
stubbing toes and cracking hips
and bending to imaginary swords.

Neurons

I'm trying to forget you
thought by slipping thought
but my neurons keep exciting
and my gut keeps getting caught

By transmitted intervention
masquerading memory
a chemical reaction
molecular machinery

I'd blame my plasma membranes
but they're doing naturally
the things that plasma membranes do
as cytoplasmic boundaries

Damn these activated receptors
and my synaptic cleft
by strengthening potentiation
without you I am bereft.

Nosebleed

I recall until my head pounds,
by the tides I shall be led
the island of your body
in the ocean of our bed

Among terraforming bedclothes
old fires leapt anew
my skin, freshly salted
by the minerals of you

Blood catches pace and thunders
seas angered and unkind,
ancient powers rise to claim
all the helpless they can find

Headlong unto the harden'd shore
in joyous, raging speed
carried into ecstasy
my nose begins to bleed

Small roses bloom upon you
bejewelling scarlet spots
I will lie here, shipwrecked,
until the pounding stops

I cannot see a single spit
of coast or island land
from the vantage point of head tipped back
ceiling sky and pinching hand

The creaking timbers echo
with the lifting of your chest
"Ssh, don't move, it's stopping"
so I close my eyes, and rest

Awakened from a slumber
without dreams or care
I find a lonely rosebud
dried within my hair

Your eyes contain the oceans
shifting immortality
your fingers are still bloodstained
salt and blood, that's you and me.

Oh!

Oh! I recall
your perfect restraint.
Sitting back on that leather,
your hands at extremes.

Oh! How I loved
the scent of your neck.
My tongue caged by teeth
longed for a taste.

Oh, you inspired me
re-created my senses.
Your aesthetic ideals
burned into my mind.

I learned
from dictated desires.
The shape of your passions,
if never your heart.

Your intensity
such visceral leanings,
exposed me and ate me
took me apart.

How I miss
your hands on my longing.
The seat of all wanting
aflame to your touch.

Oh! Such experience
a man of all things.
Take off your shirt,
let me taste you again.

Trust/love

Slowly she goes
winding her black art,
twisting the rope,
and conjuring bonds
of instant loyalty
in your close-fisted heart

Carefully she studies
adjusting the fetters,
moulding a psyche
and bending your wiles,
to her own ideals

Gently she treads
for speed is all ruinous
to this harm she does,
and sweet cruelty bestows
infinite love, between lovers.

I am

I am I am I am
floating,
sadness, floating
On a well-pool, regarding
my own face
from above

My mind, scrubbed with bleaching thoughts,
only brought you back cleaner

I am I am I am
sadness, suffocated
Holding down, holding in
I am. I am.

The Table

She set the table
and everything straight,
sent my Grandfather
to call us together
We assembled like geese
'round barley twist legs,
knees knocking,
at heights helter-skelter

Comes the fragrance of gravy
in the wake of a chicken
with a jacket bubbled and crisp
Roast potatoes, steamed windows,
an apron her gown,
she grants us with food one dear wish

This table should creak
from the weight of our smiles
and we'll leave not a morsel in sight
Her tunes carry through us
she sings us a fancy
none shall leave empty-bellied tonight

The dining room clatters
to a tune of her making
we eat in that sun-moted space
She steeps us in care
homebaked and fuss-less,
overflowing with straightforward grace

My Grandmother's house is forever
her kitchen shan't ever fall cold
Down a traceable path, food being memory,
a Dundee cake that's never grown old

The sun slides the length of that table
where I sit and write to this day
My hands feel the warmth of her dinners
and I miss her all over again.

Wake up bloodied

I dream of you, my nose bleeds
I smell metal as I wake
another feather pillow wrecked
another day to ache

I should sleep on only earth
give my essence to the ground
another link uncouples
as you the couple found

How comely of you, darling,
to pick an Essex girl
it's where I left my guts for you
mixed in with cockle shells

I shan't waste time to wonder
at the steel of your affair
curse my spiteful stomach
I cannot help to care

It twists me to oblivion
and sunders me to tears
my lower lip is bloodied
as my pillow, so I fear

Cast the feathers upwards
into the fatal blue
caught on gentle thermals
they'll find their way to you.

Whistle to the moon

All the crescent moons
all the pretty stars,
all the prisoned people
behind their prison bars,
they gape up to the heavens
and sing a song or two,
then call upon the jailer
to do what he must do.

Lupi di Lucca

The vandal princes
have broken their bonds
and this city of quiet illumination is theirs
They are roaming, slunk low,
in and out of alleyways.

Painted shadows
cast in umber and ochre
they could be
only a trick of the light.

Or a trick of the night
a man-made conjuring
in a deserted jewel box
of history.

Dashing and slipping from sight,
harmonious movement
swelling to dreaded intent.

You are the only one to see them.
Become still,
they whip soundlessly by,
rib cages grazing your thighs
Running slick as Carpathian streams,
hundreds of amber lanterns look upon you,
moonlight flashing in their mouths.

Trace a hand on their backs,
touching coarse-haired
nubs of spine.

As Romans come to hear a task
they gather, encircling
tapping claws,
above two thousand buried years.

A rippling mass of canine
puffing breath in clouds,
pulled from strange imagination
they are made flesh.

Velvet silence is broken
in lone voice
and joined, one by one.
Every snout
pointed heavenward.

And though only of six decades,
the sound, carried on Tuscan breezes,
reaches backwards through time.

Your marrow resonates,
recalling an age of beasts,
who answered to no-one,
and were not slaves to humankind.

Deep within the secret hills
beyond the safety of these walls,
their kith and kind are coming.
reborn and renewed,
and they are nine feet tall
upon their hind legs.

Living jewellery

The beetle landed on my breast
Iridescent, jade green,
tiny wings beating in time with my breathing

It shuffled around,
contemplating the pattern
of my shirt

Evidently approving
it settled, forelegs strumming
about its face, turning yellowish

I found the beetle beautifully ornamental
for a ragged old shirt
that never got dressed up.

The Black Galleon

A risen behemoth of timber, tar and nails
shredded sails
give screaming voice to nature

Loaded with salt and heartbreak,
the ship and I turn west
a bloody sun sending our faces to fire

In the hold, packed in clay
a beautiful horror sleeps
entombed twice: once for mercy
again for punishment

Heartbreak, being heavier than salt,
is our ballast
though it does not dissolve as easily.
A hellion cargo, sweeping side to side

We couldn't stay – the monster or I
there were too many nightmares
keeping us from happiness
and though we come to destitution
on a ruinous sea,
we were already broken

There comes a rush and a roar
water smashing through the decks
calls us home,
the sweetest smothering of our longing

Muscular planks of English oak
snap like matchsticks
and
we
go
down.

The final lesson

          is that

clay

dissolves

fastest

of

all.

Westgate Bay

The tide pool
a milky surface
rippled like the skin of a dead pig

Returning from a visit to my Grandmother,
trapped in respite
(no respite for the wicked she said, without humour)
Her bare room echoed
with the distinct feeling
she blames us all

Westgate Bay forgives me.
A lazy arc of pale sand
Bleeds a long promise of brighter days
into the freshening autumn chill

My Grandmother used to come here.
Inching on her two-wheeled walker,
the one with the brake and a place to sit.
Eyes milky like the tide pool,
as smiles and laughter
curled upwards with the gulls

I cannot hear the creak
of arthritic knees
above the hypnotic caress
of waves against the sea wall

All I hear
is reproach in my Grandmother's voice
when she said;
I 'had her all wrong' for suggesting
her statements of 'cannot be bothered'
and 'too much effort'
were a slap in the face of my Mother
who is constantly bothering
and making an effort
to walk in time with the beat
of two hearts:
one carefully measured

the other skipping occasionally,
thumping with fear and indignation
at infirmity
and the passing of time.

The cutting room

Humans conceive of oddities to find,
poking around inside ourselves,
halving and halving again
the capacity to store disease

We marvel at the things to be found
blooming like strange coral
in velvety recesses,
as hermit crabs, creating shelter
from our organs,
they enjoy the succour
of soft, welcoming tissue

Research falters
then gains traction
pincer'd dragging begins
and a flush of chemicals
stems the demon's fun

Diaphanous,
we wrap about what hurts us
nurturing
in deadly, unknowing love

The cutting room
is always quiet.

Pockets (a view from the wheelhouse of Covid)

Pick a little bit from the bottom of your pocket
Make a fist and hold it very tight
Grab a little courage where the fluff lives
Everything is going to be alright.

The bottom of the pocket is the safest
Curl your hand and catch your waning fight
No-one else will see the nails digging
Into your palms or knuckles turning white

Deep in the pocket's where your guts are
Look toward the dawn, here comes the light
Take hold of a fistful of pocket
And I promise you will make it through the night.

Hearts and bones

Bleached and chalky
smoothed and rough
hollowed, empty
brittle, tough

Washed up, cast out
ribs picked clean
bone encasing
a life machine.

Danny

Rise with a wave
and come down, hard,
on water as unforgiving
as a reluctant lover

Your boots were polished
shining with warm fury
and silence,
soft breezes
before a summer storm

The twist was felt, three times
hot tea burning my fingers
even with two sugars
it couldn't have been sweet

I saw you
standing at my back in the hallway mirror
reflecting everything I had dreamed
the night before

I rose, twice, on the same wave
with sore, gripping knuckles
eyes sightlessly heavenward
I churned like seaweed, and spun
outwards, upwards into space

My skin burned with your passed-on laughter
and I knew
I had forgiven because
I wished to strangle and marry you
all at once

I flicked salt-matted hair from my face
as the tide came in
swirling, rising to my knees.
I stared into the sun.
Waiting.

The old cine film

A recycled skirt of roses
cut down from sister's dress
a froth of peeping tulle
kept the war at bay

Not so much a country girl
barefoot on the sand
a hundred joyful moments
some well before their time

A song for a child not your own
bears no trace of longing
in your sunny face
or patient hands

On an open road
we watch your life begin
and see you fall in love
with your heart wide open

Big as sky, threatens to split
doubt and clouds chased away
an everlasting summer
our lives, seen backwards.

Villanelle

Check skywards, shoulder your load
rain at heel, and diving into wind
eyes forward, one foot before the other to the road

Within the patterned fields there lies a code
an ageless lesson learned in scythe and plough
check skywards once again, hitch up your load

Greet the nodding meadows come the summer
lift your knees above the winter snow
eyes forward, one foot before the other to the road

The natural paths are all but worn to nothing
there is brightness in the ways you do not know
check skywards for a third, hitch up your load

The weight of loss is lessened by a journey
it shall not matter when and where you go
eyes forward, pace forever steady on the road

No counted steps or debt for time you borrow
a witness to the seasons, breathing slow
check skywards for a fourth, lay down your load
eyes upward, standing still upon the road.

Las Vegas Wedding

The hot air cocoons us
and we drive
northwards into the heartland
of the desert

You, black shirted,
your smooth denims
an intrinsic part
of this geography,
you were born into dust

I, crisp and white,
mirrors for eyes

Your hands on the wheel
guide us into the belly of time
Intent upon a road with no end

Sunlight hitting chrome,
bleeds flashes of forever
into the gaze of those who glance upon us

The roof pulled down,
a hat is given up
to a vortex of spinning air,
whipping tiny tornadoes
of grit and long-dead weeds
into a dancing frenzy of celebration

Our fingers are gold-less
and our teeth do not itch
with the sugar of wedding cake.
Baby, never look back.

Night drive

Dusk seeps and blurs the skyline
come the close of day
a pink and lilac ribbon
heralds night unto the stage

This journey is a long one
clouds heavy, threaten rain
drops fall, refract a tiny world
get wiped away again

Yawning motorway before me
the lamps lick overhead
tarmac seams provide the beat
and keep my conscious fed

Driving through the velvet hours
with widened, tearless eyes
I could be the last one left
under orange studded skies

The rear view mirror silent
no followers in sight
the road ahead deserted
darkness left to right

The headlights kiss a pilgrimage
from Dartford all the way
up into the Highlands
where ghosts of old clans play

The cast of fading reason
blindness gives me bliss
mechanically motioned
riding the abyss

of barely wakeful notion
'cross the bones of England's spine
inverted patterns play upon
the windscreen all the time

Punctuated by reflections
blue signs winking in the black
past Sheffield, Leeds and Darlington
where I'm not going back

Driving through the darkness
steeped in rayless calm
rouged by dashboard luminesce
atramentously embalmed

A window down to rouse me
night air beholds a trace
of perfumed secrets, blown on wings
that dance about my face
'cross this scarred and sceptred landscape
not all roads lead to Rome
the bumpiest of all
are those that take us home

The snows of un-illumination
settle gently on my breast
aimed towards the mountains
running north, then turning west

Though sociable a creature
I crave no company
oneness in transition
just the road and me

Humming ceaseless through geography
resonance my friend
dreaming while I'm wide awake
from beginning until end

The shipping forecast soothes me
singing songs of gales
and this machine is my own ship
with tyres for its sails

Out upon an ocean
of blacktop, good and firm,
through slow and haunted moments
with no need to turn

One unmeasured here to there
one simple action: drive
unknowing of the distance
only sure I will arrive

And dawn will surely seek me
for now I'm content to hide
among the blessed darkness
clasped by shadow deep inside

Compelled to move forever
through ghosted, unlit time
the road ahead unhindered
the solitude sublime.

A flash that caused a panic

Collecting faults, I brandish revolt
to render this conflict all mine
walking the line, twixt aimless and random
enjoying the burn of the climb.

One in the basement, a perch on the roof
all treasures of gesture within,
wave to the postman, delivering sadness
I fall without grace into sin.

Longing for penance, taking no short cut
end-over-end go my heels,
troubled and tempered, hell lays in waiting
turning my feel into wheels.

Around the world with you

The best part of our trips was always
Clambering on and off trains,
Drinks at the airport,
Meeting in hotel lobbies
Together or apart
Travelling, functional things,
The journey to get to where you were.

The late nights, all things talked about
Clever jokes, the nuances of our friendship
A strange sort of love
Made everywhere an adventure.

The smell of travel, forget the sights,
We didn't sight-see, didn't care
For anything more than the trip
What a trip, a trip of the mind,
Precious space between
Here and there.

Vodka, and police,
The middle east, chasing drunken friends,
The hardest rain I ever felt
Recoleta, River Plate and Bar Sur
Ordering fuck-knows-what for dinner
(and not eating it)
Learning 'my husband is a gastronome' in Cantonese
And a view of a city,
Set out in ten million points of light far below me
As though it were mine to command.

Thank you for the times of my life
And damn you
For the fizzing wanderlust
That doesn't let my brain quieten

Anywhere with anyone has never been
Even half as exciting.